Explore and Draw

CARS

Ann Becker

www.rourkepublishing.com

Editor: Penny Dowdy
Art Direction: Tarang Saggar (Q2AMedia)
Designer: Neha Kaul (Q2AMedia)
Picture researcher: Mariea Janet (Q2AMedia)
Picture credits:
t=top b=bottom c=centre l=left r=right

Cover: Ariel Motor Company.
Insides: P6 : BMW Group Press Club Global, P7 : Car Culture/Corbis, P10 : Joe Robbins,
P11 : Ron Lewis/Icon SMI/Corbis, P14 : Kobal collection, P15 : Kobal collection,
P18 : BMW Group Press Club Global, P19 : Ford Motors, Folio Image : Alhovik/Shutterstock.
Q2AMedia Art Bank: Cover Page, Title Page, P4-5, P8-9, P12-13, P16-17, P20-21.

Library of Congress Cataloging-in-Publication Data
Becker, Ann, 1965 Oct. 6-
Cars : explore and draw / Ann Becker.
p. cm. – (Explore and draw)
Includes index.
ISBN 978-1-60694-349-6 (hard cover)
ISBN 978-1-60694-833-0 (soft cover)
1. Automobiles in art–Juvenile literature. 2. Drawing–Technique–Juvenile literature.
I. Title. II. Title: Explore and draw.
NC825.A8B43 2009
743'.89629222–dc22
2009021611

Printed in the USA
CG/CG

www.rourkepublishing.com - rourke@rourkepublishing.com
Post Office Box 643328 Vero Beach, Florida 32964

Contents

Technique

Before you draw cars, let's discuss shape. When you draw, you should look carefully at your **subject**. Look for simple shapes to start your drawing, and then add details to make it more realistic.

1

Look for basic shapes, such as circles, squares, rectangles, or triangles.

2

Draw the shapes you see with a very light hand.

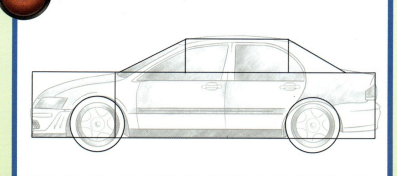

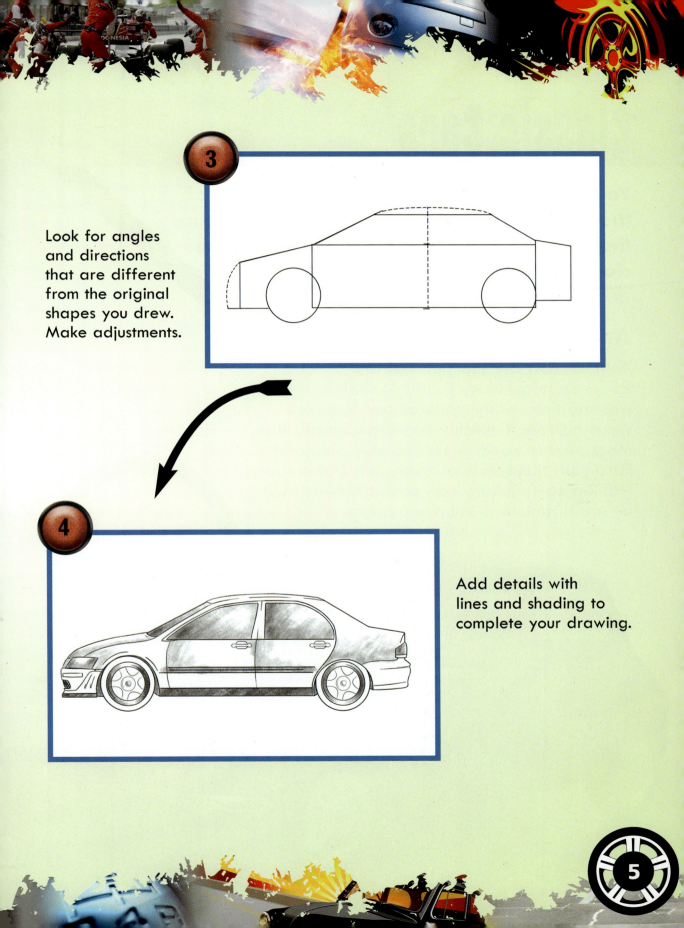

3

Look for angles and directions that are different from the original shapes you drew. Make adjustments.

4

Add details with lines and shading to complete your drawing.

Classic Cars

You can think of classic cars as the best of the best. They all have some design feature that makes them stand out. They became classics for their high quality and value.

Antique Cars

Antique cars are classics that are at least 25 years old. Henry Ford's Model T was the first really popular car. The cars were built very quickly on an **assembly line.** Most people could afford to buy one, and Ford sold thousands of them. The Duesenberg was an early luxury car. Each one was built by hand, and was very expensive.

Classic cars can be painted with traditional colors, or they can be painted for fun!

1959 - 2000

Surf Cars

Some classic car **enthusiasts** used surf cars for fun at the beach. These station wagons were called woodies, because they had wooden side panels. But the rest of the car was metal. Another popular surf car was the Volkswagen Westphalia camper. With this vehicle, you could surf all day, and then sleep in the camper!

Muscle Cars

Some people love classic cars that have power and speed. Many of these muscle cars are no longer made because they used so much gas. The Pontiac GTO had a huge engine. The Ford Mustang was smaller, but fast!

This woodie is a classic surf car.

Draw a Muscle Car

Muscle cars looked tough. Powerful engines and big wheels made these cars a hit.

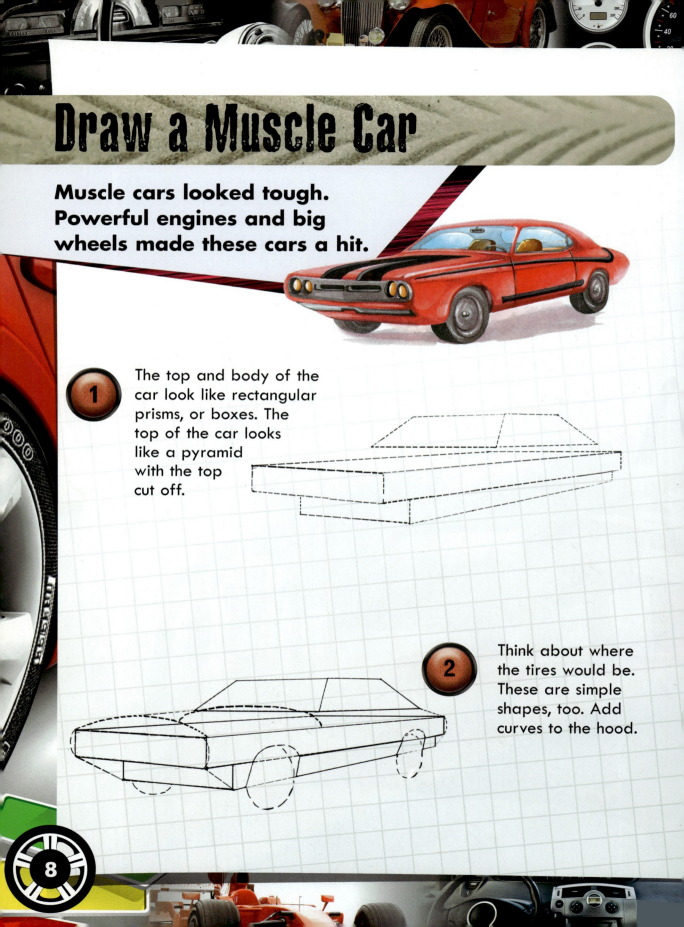

1 The top and body of the car look like rectangular prisms, or boxes. The top of the car looks like a pyramid with the top cut off.

2 Think about where the tires would be. These are simple shapes, too. Add curves to the hood.

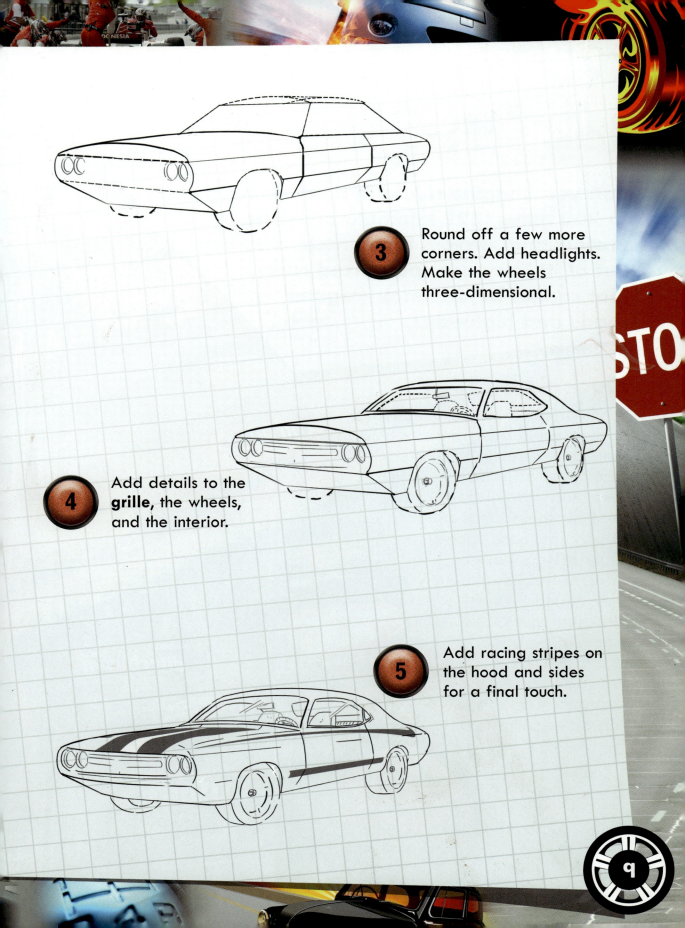

3 Round off a few more corners. Add headlights. Make the wheels three-dimensional.

4 Add details to the **grille**, the wheels, and the interior.

5 Add racing stripes on the hood and sides for a final touch.

Race Cars

Can you imagine riding in a car going close to 200 miles (322 kilometers) per hour? Professional drivers have made a career out of it! They use specialized cars that cannot be driven on regular roads and highways.

Stock Cars

Some drivers race vehicles that anyone could buy. These are cars that come directly from a car manufacturer's **stock**. In 1948, NASCAR was created to set rules for these competitions. To pay for these racers, many drivers have advertisements all over the car! Most stock car races take place in the United States. But there are some races in Australia, Canada, and other countries.

NASCAR races can be as long as 500 miles (806 kilometers), so the races last for hours.

Formula Race Cars

A Formula race car is very low to the ground. Its cockpit is only big enough for the driver. It's open to the outside air, not covered by a roof. These cars also have the wheels sticking out from the sides, instead of beneath it.

Drag Racing

If you blink, you just might miss a drag race! In this sport, two drivers race each other over a very short distance. The race is usually only a quarter mile (.4 kilometer), and it might be over in less than 20 seconds! Some of these cars have to use parachutes as part of their **braking system.**

Drag strips are short. They are usually less than a mile (1.6 kilometers) long.

Draw a Formula One Car

The first Formula One race was held in 1950. They race at over 150 miles (240 kilometers) per hour!

1 Notice the shapes that make up a Formula One car. Draw the basic shapes with a light line.

2 Change the shapes to match the car. The front end of the car is more curved than triangular.

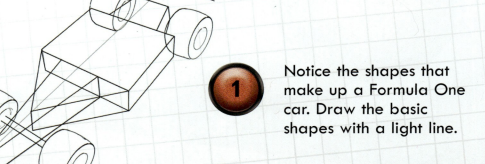

3 Add the front and rear **spoilers**.

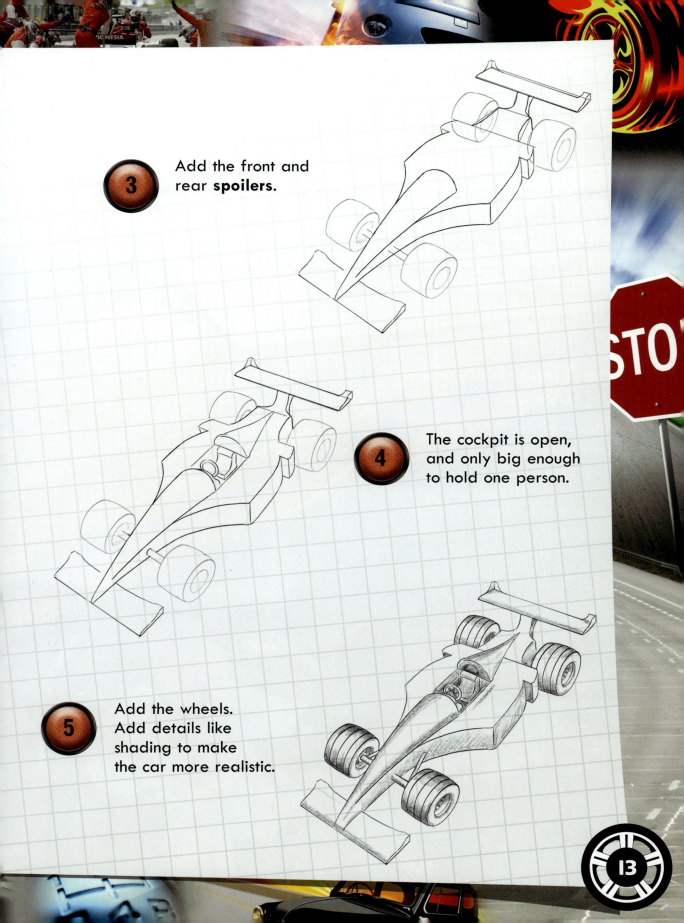

4 The cockpit is open, and only big enough to hold one person.

5 Add the wheels. Add details like shading to make the car more realistic.

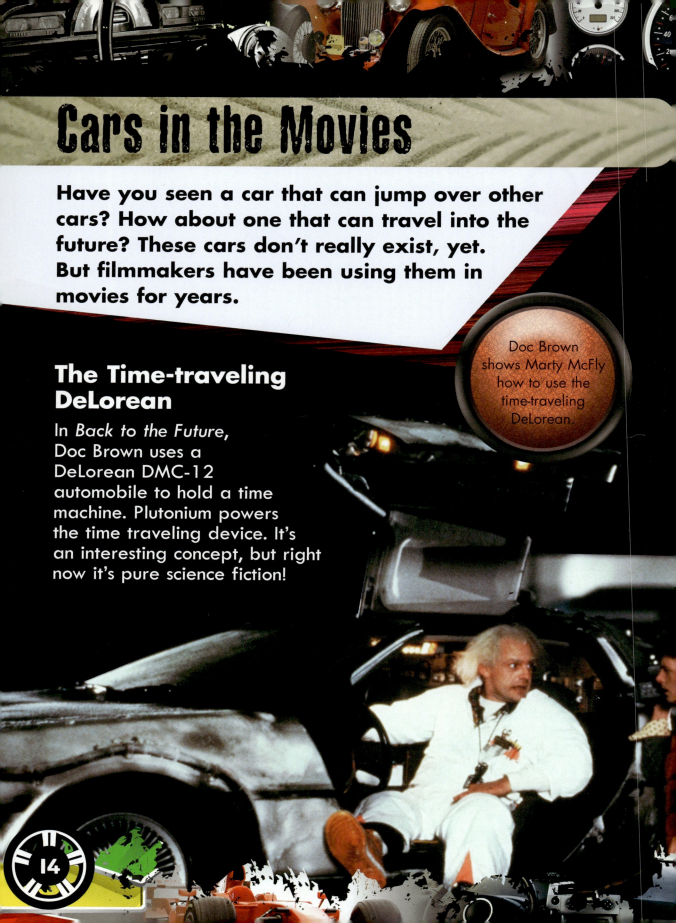

Cars in the Movies

Have you seen a car that can jump over other cars? How about one that can travel into the future? These cars don't really exist, yet. But filmmakers have been using them in movies for years.

Doc Brown shows Marty McFly how to use the time-traveling DeLorean.

The Time-traveling DeLorean

In *Back to the Future*, Doc Brown uses a DeLorean DMC-12 automobile to hold a time machine. Plutonium powers the time traveling device. It's an interesting concept, but right now it's pure science fiction!

The Batmobile

The caped crime fighter used the Batmobile to bring the bad guys to justice. His special car had armor plates to deflect bullets. It also had weapons in the front to remove obstacles in the street. It even had a small helicopter stored in the trunk!

James Bond drives an Aston Martin DBS.

James Bond's Aston Martin DB5

Unlike other movie cars, the Aston Martin DB5 was a real car. It was very popular as a luxury car in the 1960s. It was **featured** in several James Bond movies. As a spy, Bond had his own secret gadgets added to it, including rockets and bulletproof glass.

The Mach 5

The Mach 5 could do just about anything. It was a race car built by Speed Racer's father. With a push of a button, the Mach 5 could go underwater. Another button brought out steel blades to cut down trees!

Draw the Batmobile

Batman and his sidekick Robin fought crime using the Batmobile.

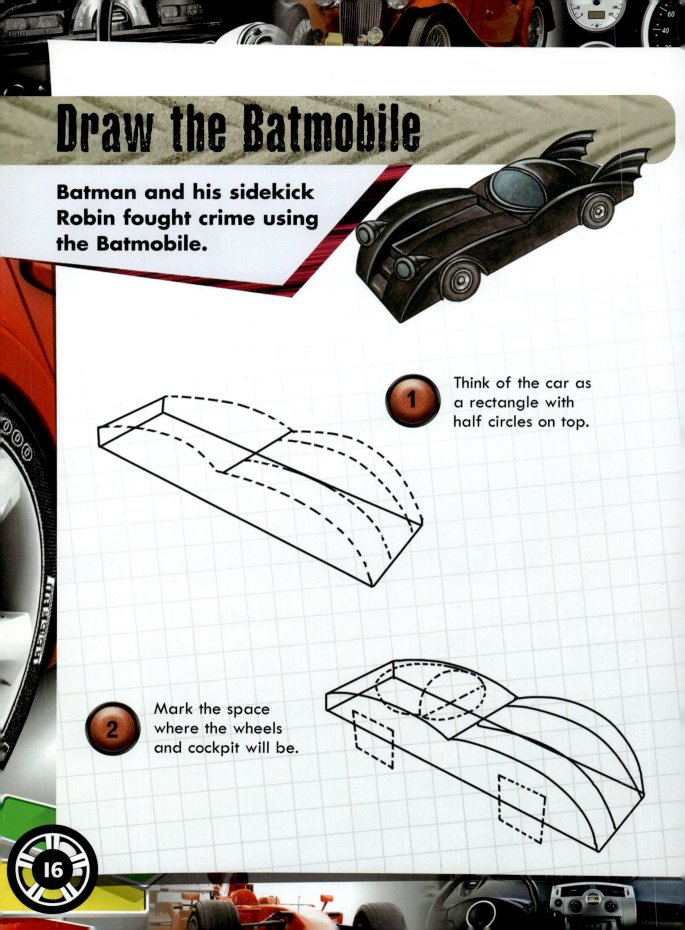

1 Think of the car as a rectangle with half circles on top.

2 Mark the space where the wheels and cockpit will be.

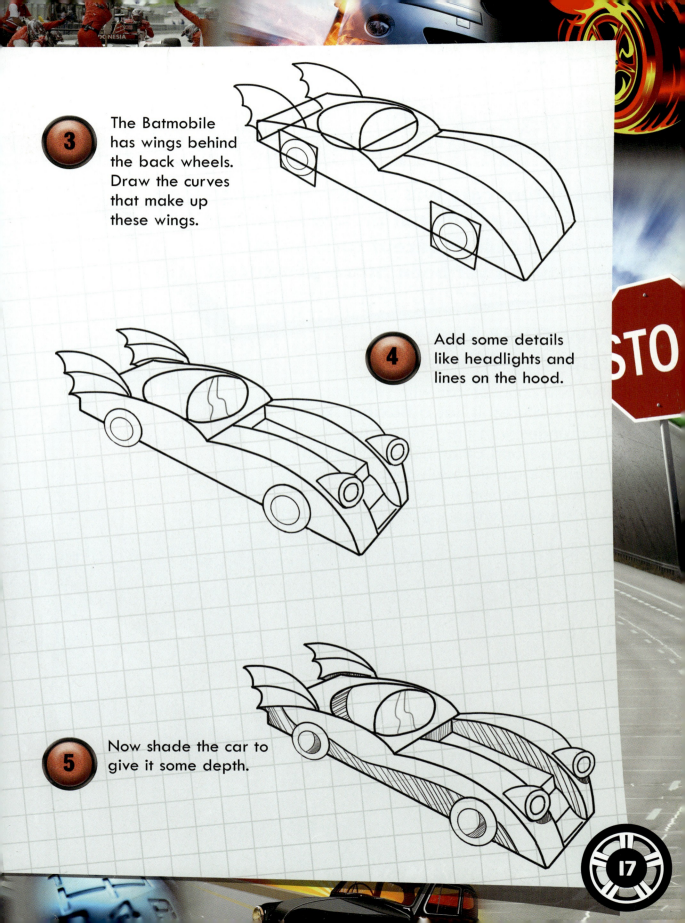

3 The Batmobile has wings behind the back wheels. Draw the curves that make up these wings.

4 Add some details like headlights and lines on the hood.

5 Now shade the car to give it some depth.

STO

17

Concept Cars

Some future cars will be able to change their shape. Others will run on hydrogen fuel. These are called concept cars, because they haven't yet been **mass-produced**.

BMW GINA Light Visionary Model

GINA is a concept car with several special features. It has a **flexible** skin that changes with the temperature, wind speed and other factors. This skin protects the car in tough conditions. It also has a steering wheel that moves out of the way when you get in the car!

The BMW Gina is covered in fabric, not metal or fiberglass.

The Airstream's doors open like a clam shell.

Ford Airstream

Ford engineers designed a car that uses electricity from hydrogen. You just plug it in to charge it! The front seats can turn completely around to face the back. It also has equipment for passengers to access the Internet and play games.

GMC Denali XT

The Denali XT combines the look of a car and a truck. It's low to the ground, but also has a bed like a pickup. It uses electricity part of the time to save on gas. This engine design is called a hybrid. In the future, most cars will be powered this way.

Draw a Denali XT

The Denali XT combines the front of a car and the back of a truck.

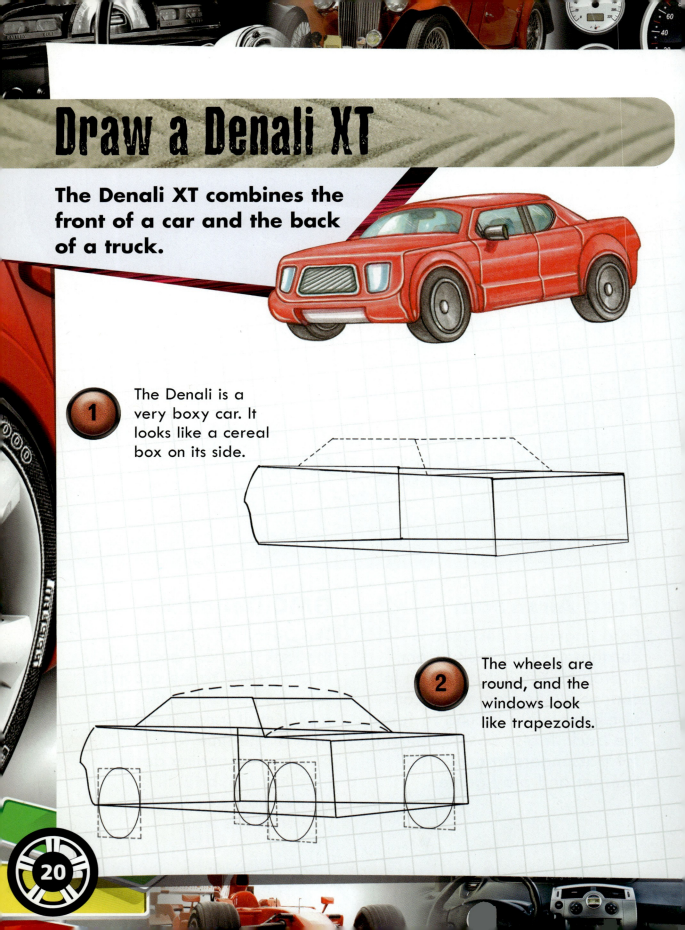

1 The Denali is a very boxy car. It looks like a cereal box on its side.

2 The wheels are round, and the windows look like trapezoids.

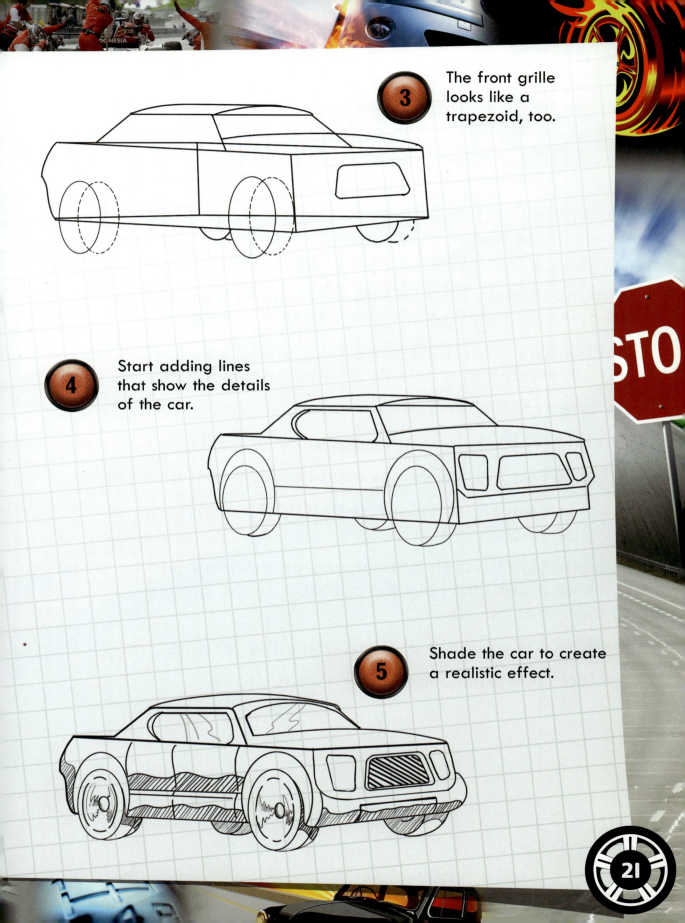

3 The front grille looks like a trapezoid, too.

4 Start adding lines that show the details of the car.

5 Shade the car to create a realistic effect.

Glossary

assembly line (uh-SEM-blee LINE): an arrangement of machines and workers in which materials pass from place to place while the item is assembled

braking system (BRAYK-ing SISS-tuhm): the parts of a vehicle that work together to stop motion

enthusiasts (en-THOO-zee-ists): people who are very interested in a certain sport, cause, or object

featured (FEE-churd): shown as an important part

flexible (FLEK-suh-buhl): able to move easily

grille (GRILL): a screen covering the front end of a car

mass-produced (MASS pruh-DOOSSD): manufactured in large quantities in a factory

spoilers (SPOIL-urs): attachments on the front and back of a car that help the car stay on the ground at high speeds

stock (STOK): supply of items available for sale

subject (SUHB-jikt): the object that is drawn

Index

Websites

http://www.aacamuseum.org/
A website for the Antique Automobile Club of America.

http://www.motortrend.com/future/concept_cars/index.html
A website from *Motor Trend Magazine* featuring designs and photos of concept cars.

http://www.imcdb.org/
The Internet movie car database lists cars that have appeared in movies by make and model.

http://musclecarfacts.net/
Information, reviews, and ratings of classic muscle cars are provided in this website.

http://www.nascar.com/
NASCAR's official website with articles, statistics, biographies of drivers, and more.

About the Author
Ann Becker is an avid reader. Ann likes to read books, magazines, and even Internet articles. She hopes that someday she will get to go on a game show and put all of that reading to good use!

About the Illustrator
Maria Menon has been illustrating children's books for almost a decade. She loves making illustrations of animals, especially dragons and dinosaurs. She is fond of pets and has two dogs named Spot and Lara. When she is not busy illustrating, Maria spends her time watching animated movies.